Mourinho

José Mourinho

headline

First published in 2015 by Headline Publishing Group

1

Cataloguing in Publication Data is available from the British Library

Hardback ISBN 978 0 7553 6553 1

E-Book ISBN 978 0 7553 6554 8

Typeset in Priori Serif and Gill Sans. Design and art direction by James Edgar at jamesedgardesign.com

Printed and bound in Italy by Rotolito Lombarda S.p.A.

Headline's policy is to use papers that are natural, renewable and recyclable products and made from wood grown in sustainable forests. The logging and manufacturing processes are expected to conform to the environmental regulations of the country of origin.

Headline Publishing Group
Carmelite House
50 Victoria Embankment
London EC4Y 0DZ

www.headline.co.uk
www.hachette.co.uk

CONTENTS

INTRODUCTION

It's very hard for me to put my fifteen years as a manager into words – the pivotal moments, my emotions, my memories. But images make it easier – images that I keep in my heart, in my soul, images that let me dive into these moments and talk about them like they happened yesterday.

There have been so many books written by people that don't even know me, so many books full of untrue comments, so many books so far away from what I think, what I feel and who I am.

I can be emotional. I can cry with victories, I can smile with defeats.

In the victories I think about my family's happiness, I enjoy my players' pride, I feel the supporters' ecstasy. In defeat I can smile because I want the next match, because the reaction will make me better and stronger, because I know that a defeat for me is the start of another winning period.

Moments, feelings, memories, emotions – this is my career, this is what I want to share, and the best way to do it is through few words and great images.

From Portugal, England, Italy and Spain – A Liga, the Premier League, il Scudetto, La Liga, A Taça de Portugal, the FA Cup and the League Cup, Coppa Italia and Copa del Rey, Supertaça de Portugal, the Community Shield, Supercoppa Italiana, Supercopa de España, the UEFA Cup and Champions League...thank you football for making my childhood dreams come true, but more than that – thank God for the family I have.

This is my picture book...

SL BENFICA

2000

Head coach for the first time
at Benfica.

I was ready. I was ready to make
an impact, I was ready to cope with
the responsibility, but the club
wasn't ready for me.

It was a difficult period for this
giant club, financially in trouble,
an election period in a presidentialist
club — there was great instability.
But what an experience for me,
and what a memory! My last match
was the Lisbon derby: Benfica 3,
Sporting 0.

UNIÃO DE LEIRIA
2001–2002

Next step – Leiria. It was a small club and I had clear objectives: not to be relegated, to work and develop players, sell some others. It was an important experience for me, and a great motivation to do something special. Perhaps too special, too fast!

I arrived in July 2001; by December
Leiria was third in the Portuguese
league and I already had Benfica and
Porto fighting for me. Benfica's new
president wanted me back to restart
my work with a 'new' club in search
of institutional stability.
FC Porto's president was incredible
in his approach. He said: 'Mourinho,
you are the man for a new Porto, what
incentive can I give you to to come?'
I wanted nothing. It was enough to
know I was the man they wanted.

My last training session at Leiria.
I think they knew what they were
doing – throwing me to the world.
I left in January 2001 – by May 2002
I was Portuguese champion, by May
2003 I was a UEFA Cup winner, by
May 2004 I was European champion.

FC PORTO
2002–2004

I arrived at Porto and in my
presentation I told the press:
'Next season we will be champions.'
The pressure was on my shoulders.
The only solution was to work better
and harder than anyone else.

One year later, I had won my first championship. This was our last match at home vs Sporting Lisbon. A blue celebration with white hair? Well, I was trying to imagine me ten years later.

A celebration? No ... just a visit to the thousands of Porto supporters waiting for more than 48 hours to try and get a ticket to the UEFA Cup Final in Sevilla. As they slept and ate in the queue, dreaming about a seat in Sevilla, I visited them, I took some drink and food for them. They were amazingly passionate people. I loved to work for them.

Sevilla. The UEFA Cup Final against Celtic. It was an amazing football match. After 90 minutes the score was 2–2 and we were heading for extra time. These were important minutes. We needed a game plan for the last, crucial 30 minutes. It's incredible to see their attentiveness, incredible the way they are concentrating on my words. Seven of these players are now football managers. Legacy? Or just coincidence?

The game finishes 3–2 after extra time, and I have my first European trophy. I will never forget it. We landed in Porto and we went directly to our stadium. At 4 a.m. it was full! That's passion. I liked that feeling of making others happy, but I wanted more ...

And a week later, I got my wish.
The Portuguese cup final – three
titles in a couple of weeks. A team
of babies won the treble ... players
who had come from the youth team,
players I brought from Leiria,
players we bought from small
Portuguese clubs, players without
titles, players ready to work, fight
for success, for their future.
An amazing team, a team that
might have been destroyed,
but the president fought to keep it
intact. 'Mourinho, don't leave Porto,
stay one more season, I promise
I won't sell one single player, let's
dream about the Champions League.'
I decided to stay ... and we did dream.

Portuguese champions again in 2004, and a strange experience because Sporting drew and we celebrated the title in the hotel before we played our game the next day. Two minutes after the final whistle of the Sporting game, the square by the hotel became blue and white. We went to the windows and balconies: champagne, happiness and more champagne. We had won our second league title in two seasons.

We were also enjoying our Champions League run as outsiders. In the first knock-out stage we beat Manchester United at home, 2–1. And then my first visit to Old Trafford, the theatre of dreams – why not make your dreams come true? A last-minute goal … why not celebrate it this way? This is surely an iconic picture in my career. A 50-metre sprint at Old Trafford. The next day I had two big English clubs knocking on my door. A blue and a red.

Players, subs, manager, flag!
Madness, but madness from
our hearts.

Gelsenkirchen. The Champions League Final, 26 May 2004. Porto vs Monaco. I prepared every detail of our game plan, but more than that I had to prepare myself. I needed emotional balance, emotional control, in a game that wasn't just a game. This was a Champions League for me, for us, for Porto, for Portugal. This was our history. When we scored the third goal my mask disappeared. I don't need to look at books to remember these players: Vítor Baía, Paulo Ferreira, Ricardo Carvalho, Jorge Costa, Nuno Valente, Costinha, Pedro Mendes, Maniche, Deco, Derlei, Carlos Alberto. And on the bench: Nuno, Ricardo Costa, José Bosingwa, Pedro Emanuel, Dmitri Alenichev, Edgaras Jankauskas, Benni McCarthy. Thirteen Portuguese players — eleven of whom arrived at the club in my period there.

Before the game, in the press
conference, she was on the table and
I refused to touch or even look at her.
After the game, in the dressing room,
I got her, and I keep this picture
hidden in my memories.

They were there! I couldn't see my family in the stadium, but I felt their presence all the time. I had won a Champions League with a Portuguese team less than four years after the start of my managerial career. But while all this crossed my mind in the last moments of the game, I was still thinking – they are here! This picture means the world.

After the final we flew in to Porto.
Here I am hand-in-hand with
Matilde, holding the match ball.
History made, two days later
we flew to London.

CHELSEA FC

2004–2008

I landed in London with pressure
on my shoulders again. I had said
at my Porto press conference
'next season we are going to be
champions', and this time there
was a pearl for the English media:
'I am a special one.' Pressure?
Yes, but positive pressure. Let's go!

A few months later we were in the
League Cup Final against Liverpool.
It was 1–1 at full-time and here
I'm saying: 'Calm down because
the game isn't over. We have extra
time to play.'

The League Cup. My first title with Chelsea. It was the first title for the owner, and the feeling was that this was just the beginning.

Almost 50 years later, Chelsea FC
are League Champions again!
My third championship in three
consecutive years. We clinched the
Premier League title after victory
at Bolton – these were emotional
scenes with the Chelsea family.

At half-time I told my players:
'Make sure the next time you put
a foot in this dressing room you
are champions, make sure you
don't wait for next week. It's here,
it's now, go and win.' They did it.

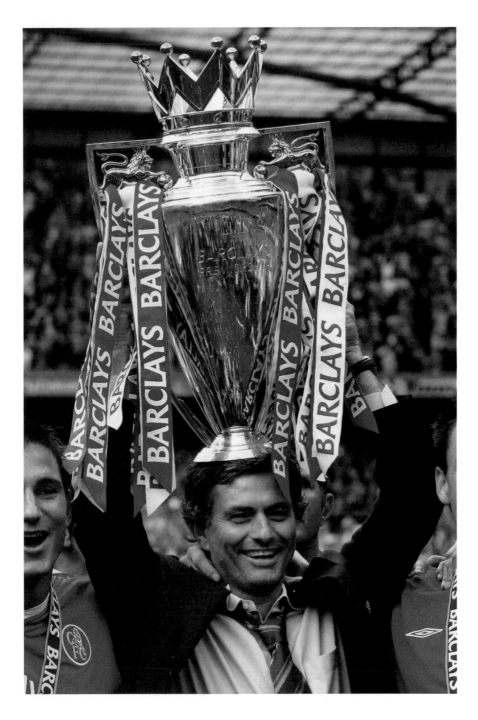

Champions at Bolton, lifting the cup
at Stamford Bridge.

We were loving our life in England.

...my family was happy.

Sir Bobby Robson awarding me
the UEFA Coach of the Year Award
at Stamford Bridge.

With Chelsea supporters there was passion from day one.

My second season in charge
starts with the Community Shield,
and victory over Arsenal.

Relations with the players
were phenomenal.

Pelé presented me with the award
at the BBC Sports Personality of
the Year ceremony.

Our second Premier League was arriving and with a record points tally – one that is still in place to this day.

A 3–0 victory over Manchester
United gave me my fourth
championship in a row.

The 2006/2007 season. Another
League Cup title, but a draw at
Arsenal stopped our dream of the
treble. But even in defeat we were
a team, even in defeat we had pride,
even in defeat we were preparing
for the next victory.

A couple of weeks later we played
in the first FA Cup Final at the
new Wembley stadium, against
Manchester United, and completed
the set of English trophies. In three
seasons we won everything. Another
extra time, another magic moment.
It was the 119th minute and Drogba
scored. It was an honour to lift the
cup in front of Prince William.

I was so happy to walk up the iconic stairs. How many times as a kid had I watched FA Cup Finals? This time it was me coming back down with the trophy. Amazing.

When Chelsea and I ended our contract in September of the 2007/2008 season, the fans couldn't believe it. Here they show their feelings with a banner on the Fulham Road. I left, but I always felt that I would return.

INTER MILAN
2008–2010

After Chelsea and English football,
I wanted more. I wanted a different
football culture, a new challenge,
and, if possible, a difficult one.
Mr Moratti and Inter Milan had
a dream for almost fifty years, to be
European champions. I knew I would
have to study the league, know every
detail about the teams and players,
and learn the language. Once more
I was ready, once more my family was
open to a new adventure.

With Eusébio, the most important
sportsman in our country's history.
As manager of Inter we won the
first Eusébio Cup (a pre-season
tournament held annually in his
honour), and Mr Moratti told me,
'Keep the cup, José, I know what
he means to you.'

In my first season in Italy we won
the Italian Supercup with victory
against Roma, and here we are
celebrating winning the league.
It was a Scudetto that we dominated
in a comfortable way.

With my assistant Rui Faria. What
do we need to have a chance in the
Champions League? We thought,
we discussed, we analysed, we
projected, and once more we dreamt.

The more we were focused on our Champions League dream, the more difficulties we had in the Italian league. We suffered a couple of defeats, Roma were pushing hard. I felt mistake after mistake was being made against us by officials. At one period I was training 11v10 so many times for when one of our players got sent off, but I forgot 11v9. It happened on this day against Sampdoria when two of my players were sent off.

We reached the last sixteen of the
Champions League knock-out
stages, only to be drawn with Chelsea!
It was so difficult – my Inter against
my Chelsea. And Chelsea was literally
my Chelsea – the players I loved,
the team I had built. Stamford Bridge
– my stadium, the stadium where
I never lose. The final score was
Chelsea 0 Inter 1. It felt like Inter
had broken a psychological wall
where before they had continually
failed in the Champions League.
In March we found ourselves top
of the league, in the quarter-finals
of the Champions League and in the
quarter-finals of the Italian cup.

A special number ten. Adapted to
play in a 4–3–3 and a 4–4–2. He
made the difference when it came to
the strategies needed for Champions
League games. Here the result was
Inter Milan 3, Barcelona 1.

The Champions League. The best team in the world came to the San Siro and lost 3–1. In the second leg in Barcelona we had a dream, but they had an obsession. We wanted to win the Champions League but they wanted to win the Champions League in the Santiago Bernabéu Stadium. In the second leg in Barcelona, after only a few minutes we were down to ten men. It seemed like an impossible mission, but we were ready for everything. We were experienced at playing with ten men. We had great defensive organisation, a clear game plan, big hearts, and we were ready to sweat blood. We lost 1–0 but won 3–2 on aggregate. Inter was in the Madrid final...

We arrived at Milan airport after
knocking Barça out to be met with
a great sense of anticipation as we
prepared for the end of the season.
Like the supporters, we were feeling
unbeatable, we were feeling that the
best was to come...

Two weeks to the end of the season,
three matches to play: the cup final
against Roma in the Stadio Olimpico,
the last league match in Siena where
Inter needed to win to be champions
and, a few days later, Inter v Bayern
Munich in Madrid in the Champions
League Final.
1! Coppa Italia: Roma 0 Inter 1.

2! Scudetto: Siena 0, Inter 1.

And 3! Champions League:
Bayern Munich 0, Inter 2.
My town and my people were
in Madrid.

With Louis van Gaal. To manage
a team in a Champions League Final
against him was strange – to fight
for the biggest prize against a friend
wasn't easy, but that's football.

We were ready. We won even before
the kick-off. The Interista family
played their part. And that cup was
ours, that cup was flying to Milan.
Il Duomo was burning and waiting
for us.

It was like I was playing – here I stopped Robben from taking a fast throw-in.

Celebrating our second goal.

The final whistle. My last match
with Inter. The biggest prize.
Too much!

My captain.

I needed to find my family.

My flag.

People like him make Inter's history.

With President Moratti.
This was his dream.

I needed a shower.

My boy was also emotional with
our second Champions League.

Our dream, my ball, our cup, my team: Júlio César, Maicon, Lúcio, Samuel, Chivu, Zanetti, Cambiasso, Eto'o, Sneijder, Pandev and Milito. On the bench were Toldo, Córdoba, Mariga, Stanković, Muntari, Balotelli, Materazzi – and Motta suspended. After refusing Real Madrid twice, it was time to go and try to be the first person to win the Premier League, Scudetto and La Liga.

Following page: Il Duomo

REAL MADRID CF
2010–2013

With the FIFA World Coach of
the Year award. After winning the
treble with Inter I would have been
an easy choice.

I was emotional, and in a flash
I can remember all I got through
to be there and be elected the best
manager in the world.

Breaking Barcelona's dominance
was difficult but I felt passionate
about the task. Real Madrid is a huge
club, but it wasn't easy. I gave all
I had, I worked harder than ever.
Again I won every competition
in a new country: La Liga (with
a record 100 points and 121 goals),
Copa del Rey (for the first time in
eighteen years) and the Spanish
Supercup, beating Barcelona in the
final. We were so close to reaching
the Champions League Final, but we
were eliminated by Bayern Munich.
In the first leg we conceded in the last
minute and in the second we missed
three penalties in the shoot-out.

For sure I was losing!

A great final (and another one
that went to extra time) in Valencia
as we beat Barcelona to win the
Copa del Rey.

On the flight with the trophy.

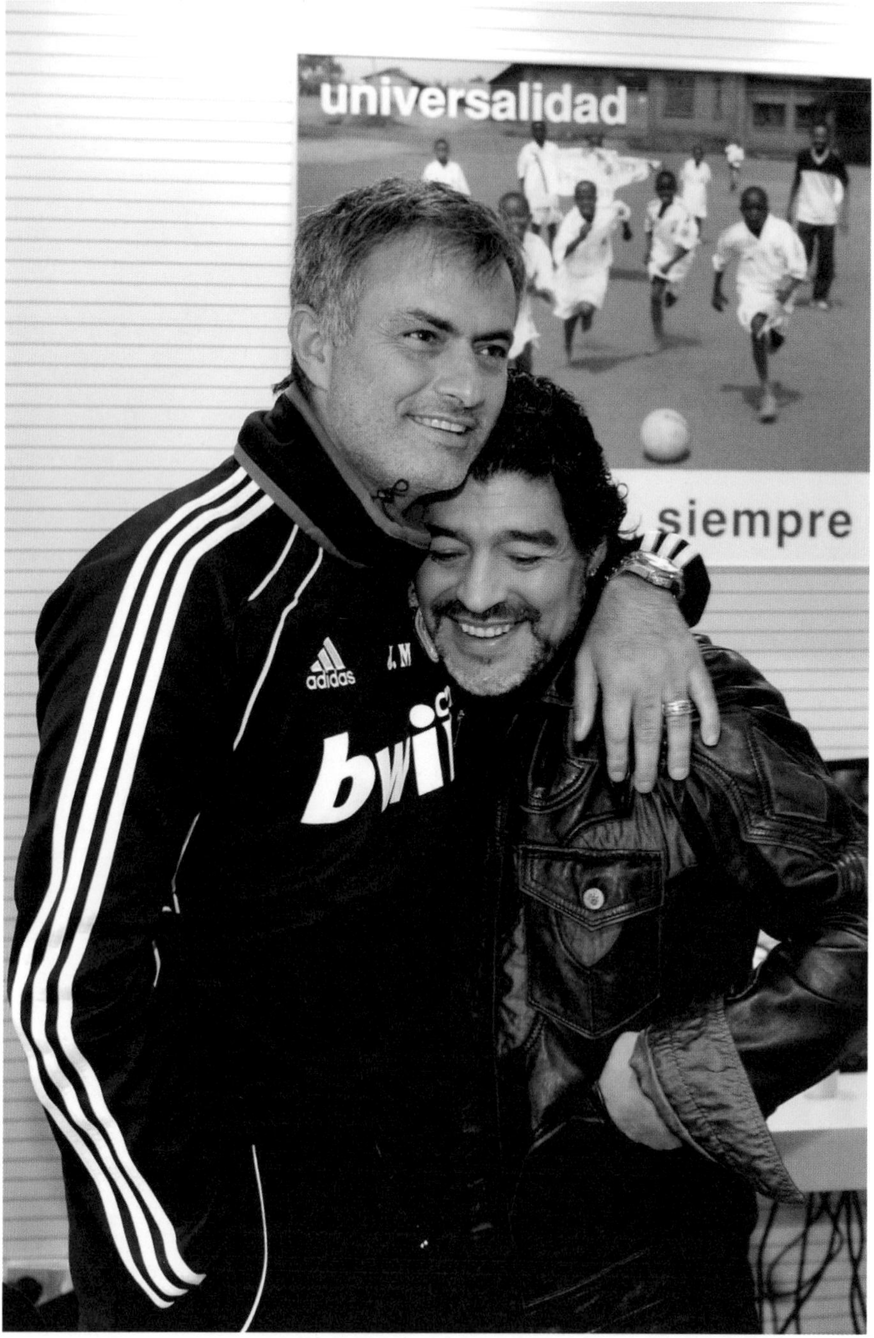
universalidad
siempre
adidas
J.M
bwi

A special visit.

With Don Alfredo Di Stéfano as he
presented me with the Spanish Coach
of the Year award.

We were virtually champions
in the Camp Nou with a 3–1 victory,
but we were mathematically
champions two weeks later in
the cathedral of Bilbao...

Seven league titles and the only
person to be a champion in England,
Spain and Italy, as well as Portugal.
That's the reason for the big smile.

Following page:
On the podium to receive the
La Liga Trophy.

As always: my passion, my support, my happiness.

**A different shirt to Inter, but the
same smile and happiness.**

We made history when we reached
100 points on the way to winning
La Liga in 2012.

An amazing club. Madrid stopped
to celebrate the title.

My last game against the boss at
Old Trafford. We beat United 2–1 in
the last 16 of the Champions League,
in March 2013. A special man, a
special opponent, a special friend.

My office. So many hours of work,
one last trophy – the Super Cup.
A moment to be happy again.
Happiness isn't all about winning.
Happiness is smiling a lot, and being
surrounded by people you love at
home, by people you like in your
work. It was time to be happy again.
There were different options, but
only one decision for my family.
England, London, Chelsea FC.
Tradition says: 'Don't go back to a
club where you were happy before.'
Perfect – another challenge is exactly
what I wanted!

CHELSEA FC

2013–Present

Chelsea, again.

I knew that one day I would be back. Back to rebuild, back to end an era, back to start a new team with new players with the same ambitions, and win again!

I was awarded the Football Writers'
Tribute Award at the FWA Awards.

Being one of the fans makes me
live my job in a different way.
It's a positive – it means I am
more than just a manager.

This is exactly the way I feel it.
Not just the Chelsea manager,
but one of them.

And they knew it. They knew that
I was one of them. Back to stay,
back to give my talent, my work,
but also my passion.

31 December, midnight. Only in
England could I be celebrating
the new year in the team hotel ...
drinking tea! The first season
was the season of the 'almost'.
Almost champions, almost there.
But it was also the season of the
rebuild. The 'pre-season' of a
successful season – 2014/2015.

I was so proud to win the best manager in the history of Portuguese football award for the centenary of the Portuguese FA. There are no words! It was such an honour, such a moment, in front of all the important people in the history of Portuguese football, to win this award.

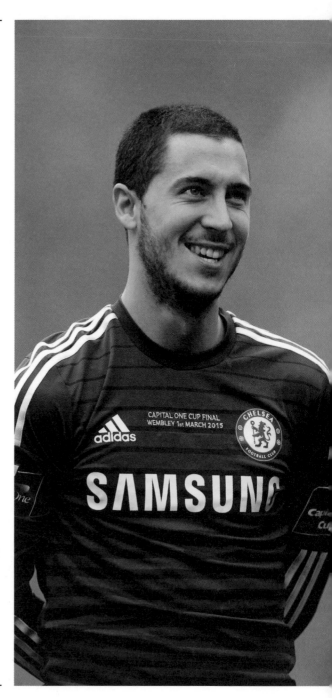

Before the final, before the national anthem. What are these two laughing at? I was telling him that I was desperate to start the game, but if I played instead of being the manager I would be off within five minutes. 'Why boss, injured?' he said. And I answered him: 'No, with a red card; with the adrenaline I have, I would have ended up kicking someone!'

1 March, 2015. The League Cup
Final. Back to Wembley, back to
win. After finals against Manchester
United, Liverpool and Arsenal,
this time it was another London rival
in Tottenham. A kiss to my family.
We were ninety minutes away
from our first trophy of the season.

I was really happy to win the League
Cup. Our work was getting results.

A first cup for these boys, a first
cup for me in my second period
at Chelsea.

Six kids ... or six plus an old kid!
Football gets the best out of us.
I always say: enjoy it, boys, because
it is so hard to win that you have to
enjoy it when you do.

The Premier League was almost ours. Almost... almost... But football isn't about almost, it's about doing it. 3 May 2015. Chelsea vs Crystal Palace. Three points and a fourth Premier League for Chelsea. Three points and my third Premier League. Three points and my eighth league title in four different countries. The last minute. I'm gesturing to Didi to say 'hold the ball, run the clock down.' My son is feeling the pressure of the moment, my daughter hides behind the TV camera, my wife waits for the last whistle.

A throw-in in the Palace half.
No time for more danger. Champions!

No cup – not yet! It was our fault for being champions before the last match... But this is a really a special picture in my office at Stamford Bridge a couple of minutes after the game. A special photo, a special family. We left Portugal in 2004 and we are having a phenomenal adventure. Different countries, different clubs, different schools, different teachers and friends, but always a great family. Without them and their unconditional support, I couldn't have had the career I have had. I owe them that.

After the title victory, the hangover
and a defeat to West Brom, it was
important to remember we were still
number one, we were champions,
we were special. One finger says it all.

24 May, 2015, Stamford Bridge. They are relaxed, but not me. We are champions but we have a last game at home before we receive the cup. The day won't have the same taste without a victory – we have to win. I have one defeat in 99 Premier League matches at home. The *Guinness Book of Records* have just informed me about the record and this moment is really one that means a lot – in England, in the most difficult and competitive championship in world football. Ninety-nine matches at Stamford Bridge with only one defeat – with a penalty that was never a penalty!

A testimonial for the champions
of 2004/2005. A great moment
to be reunited with my players.
Many of them are retired from
football, others are starting a
managerial career, but in football
friends stay forever.

A great day. Medals around
our necks, the cup in our hands.

As Rui Faria said to me, this was a day to enjoy, but also a day to think about what made us champions, so we know how to repeat it.

**Eight league titles – I still have two
fingers available!**

Previous page:
Watching them is watching
happiness. It was the first title
for many, one more unforgettable
moment from the side.

Left:
And now I can leave from the
back of the celebrations with
the feeling of 'job done'.

My wife, my daughter, my son.
Their cup.

Enjoying the parade.

A super shirt.

The end of the season. Tired?
Definitely, yes. But in one week
I'll be ready for more!

APPENDIX

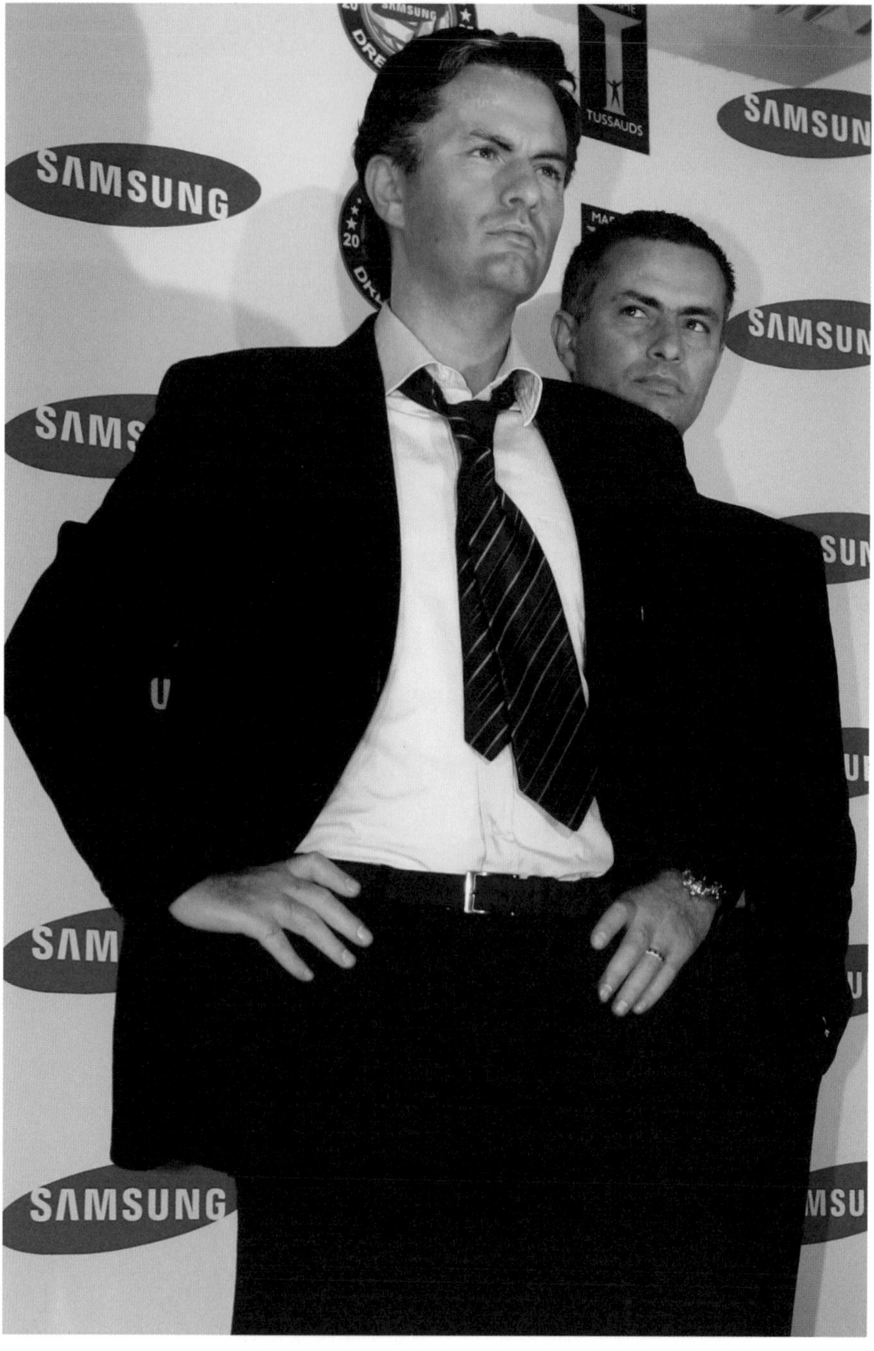
TUSSAUDS
SAMSUNG
SAMSUNG

Madame Tussauds in London.
A football manager? This was
a surprise, and also an honour.

In Portugal. It was a great honour
to receive the *Ordem do Infante*.
It was also a responsibility I feel
every day, especially representing
my country abroad.

Football gave me a lot — pride,
honour and the possibility to do good,
to help people. It was heartbreaking
to meet these kids. So hard, but a
beautiful feeling to attract people's
attention and support for these
causes. And all of them I met over
the years are so beautiful.

A visit to Israel and Palestine...
Coach for Peace. Playing with kids,
meeting politic power. Can football
unite people? Yes.

Academy football in Africa: Senegal,
Ghana, Ivory Coast. I feel their dream
and support them. Beautiful.

I am a WFP Ambassador. I feel
so proud of it and thankful to
football for allowing me this status
and being able to have a positive
social influence.

Doctor Honoris Causa in my
FMH Sports University in Lisbon.
My parents' pride with my career
is a great feeling for a son.

With the World Food Programme
in the Ivory Coast. A unique feeling,
facing the sad reality. I want to help,
I want to be a voice.

Setúbal, my city. I was given this award by the mayor. I couldn't be there because it was a match day, but my wife and little daughter received it. In 2013 they named a road after me: José Mourinho Avenue. My city is always proud of my career. And I am always José from Setúbal.

Soccer Aid uses football to help
people. I am always happy to do it.

Players' kids are always welcome in our space.

Twenty-second, but not the last...